The Real World of Pirates

PIRATE TREASURE

STOLEN RICHES

By Liam O'Donnell

Consultant:
Sarah Knott, Director
Pirate Soul Museum
Key West, Florida

Capstone
press®

Mankato, Minnesota

Edge Books are published by Capstone Press,
151 Good Counsel Drive, P.O. Box 669, Mankato, Minnesota 56002.
www.capstonepress.com

Library of Congress Cataloging-in-Publication Data
O'Donnell, Liam, 1970–
    Pirate treasure: stolen riches / by Liam O'Donnell.
    p. cm.—(Edge Books. The real world of pirates)
    Summary: "Describes the things that pirates considered treasure, how they got
their treasure, and what they did with it"—Provided by publisher.
    Includes bibliographical references and index.
    ISBN-13: 978-0-7368-6428-2 (hardcover)
    ISBN-10: 0-7368-6428-8 (hardcover)
    1. Pirates—Juvenile literature. 2. Capture at sea—Juvenile literature.
3. Treasure-troves—Juvenile literature. I. Title. II. Series.
G535.O375 2007
910.4'5—dc22   2006006998

Editorial Credits
Angie Kaelberer, editor; Thomas Emery, designer; Tom Alvarado, illustrator;
    Kim Brown, colorist; Wanda Winch and Charlene Deyle, photo researchers

Photo Credits
Corbis/Bettmann, 8, 12
Getty Images Inc./Hulton Archive, 16
Image courtesy of Etty van Urk, 28
North Wind Picture Archives, 25
Peter Newark's American Pictures, 4; Historical Pictures, 7, 15, 19, 22
Rick Reeves, 20
Shutterstock/Andres Rodriguez, 6
SuperStock, 11; Harold M. Lambert, 27

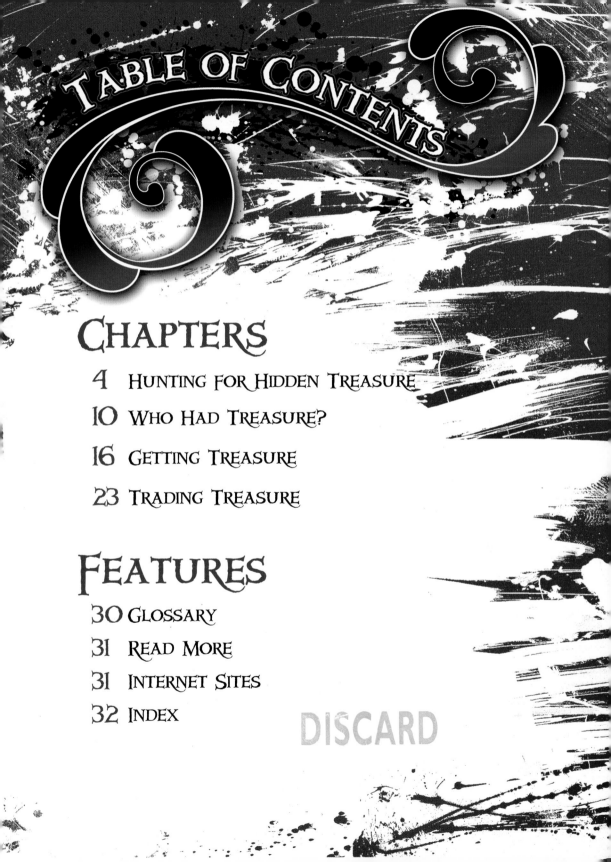

TABLE OF CONTENTS

CHAPTERS

FEATURES

DISCARD

Chapter One

HUNTING FOR HIDDEN TREASURE

For centuries, people have searched Oak Island for buried pirate treasure.

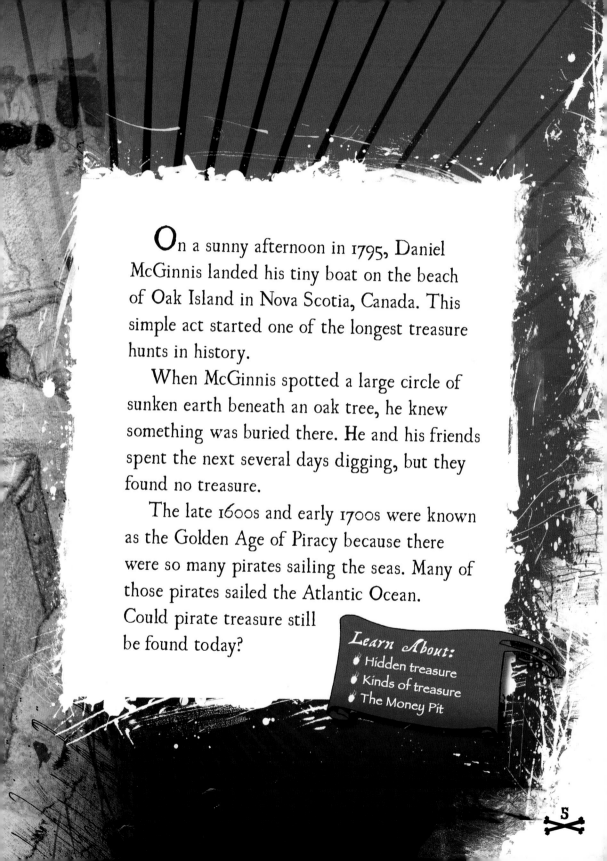

On a sunny afternoon in 1795, Daniel McGinnis landed his tiny boat on the beach of Oak Island in Nova Scotia, Canada. This simple act started one of the longest treasure hunts in history.

When McGinnis spotted a large circle of sunken earth beneath an oak tree, he knew something was buried there. He and his friends spent the next several days digging, but they found no treasure.

The late 1600s and early 1700s were known as the Golden Age of Piracy because there were so many pirates sailing the seas. Many of those pirates sailed the Atlantic Ocean. Could pirate treasure still be found today?

Learn About:
* Hidden treasure
* Kinds of treasure
* The Money Pit

Robbers on the Sea

Many people think of pirate treasure as gold and jewels. Most often, though, pirates stole everyday items. Their loot could be bales of cotton, barrels of tobacco, extra sails, or tools. These things were not as exciting as chests of gold, but they were still valuable. Cotton, tobacco, sails, and tools could all be sold for money. Making money was every pirate's goal.

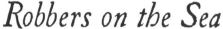

Everyday items were just as valuable to pirates as gold coins or glittering jewels.

Human Treasure

Even people could be treasure. Pirates sometimes kidnapped ship doctors, carpenters, and navigators. These skilled workers were worth their weight in gold to a pirate crew.

Slaves were also considered treasure. European sailors captured people in Africa. The sailors brought the Africans to other countries, where they were sold to the highest bidder. Slaves were forced to work long hours for their owners without pay. Sometimes, though, pirates asked slaves they captured to join their crews. These slaves became free men.

Some captains used slaves as manpower for their ships.

To pirates, stealing treasure wasn't wrong. They did it to survive.

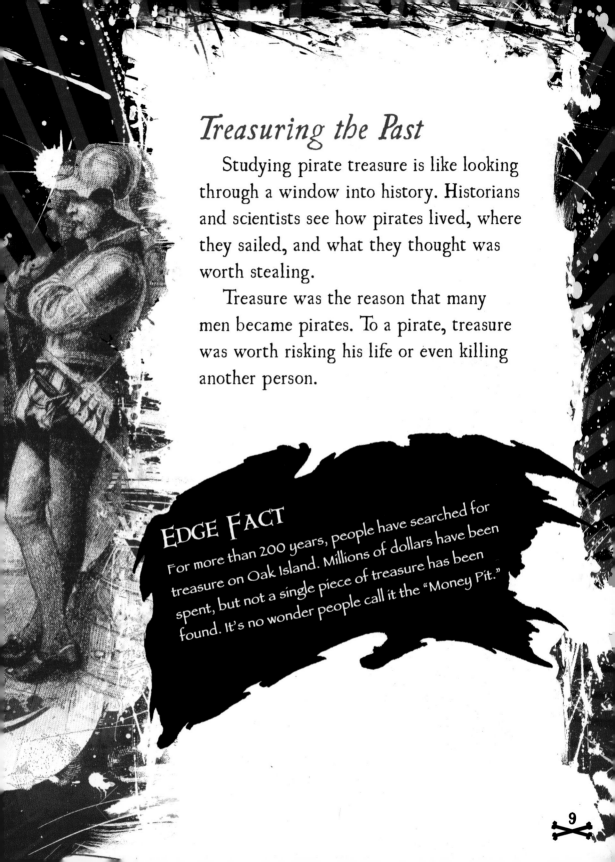

Treasuring the Past

Studying pirate treasure is like looking through a window into history. Historians and scientists see how pirates lived, where they sailed, and what they thought was worth stealing.

Treasure was the reason that many men became pirates. To a pirate, treasure was worth risking his life or even killing another person.

Edge Fact

For more than 200 years, people have searched for treasure on Oak Island. Millions of dollars have been spent, but not a single piece of treasure has been found. It's no wonder people call it the "Money Pit."

Chapter Two

WHO HAD TREASURE?

Before there were planes or trains, the only way to move things over long distances was by ship. Ships filled with gold, spices, and jewels sailed across the seas.

Items carried by ships were called cargo. A ship's cargo could be worth a lot of money. Getting it was a pirate's chance to be rich.

Learn About:
- Spread of piracy
- The Great Mogul
- Pirates of the Red Sea

Large merchant ships were
usually loaded with cargo.

11

By law, only British ships could bring goods to the American colonies.

Natural Treasure Chest

Several events helped spread piracy. In the 1600s, England started colonies in North America. The new colonies were full of lumber, wildlife, and minerals.

The English government wanted to control the colonies and their resources. Only English ships were allowed to transport goods to and from the colonies. The colonists could sell their products only to the English. Colonists had to accept whatever the English charged or paid them.

Pirates decided to give the English some competition. For a time, both pirates and colonists benefited. Pirates had a market for their stolen loot. The colonists could buy goods at lower prices than the English charged.

Tew's Treasure Hunt

Laws helped spread piracy, but so did the possibility of becoming rich. In 1692, Captain Thomas Tew planned to sail his ship the *Amity* from the Caribbean island of Bermuda to Africa. Tew's mission was to raid a French fort for the English government.

A few days into the journey, Tew suggested to his crew that they search for treasure. The crew agreed. They steered the ship away from Africa and started searching for merchant ships to rob. Tew and his crew became pirates.

A few months later, the *Amity* crew successfully raided a ship on the Red Sea. The ship belonged to Aurangzeb, also known as the Great Mogul. The Great Mogul's empire stretched across Asia. The ship held enough gold and jewels to make Tew and his men rich.

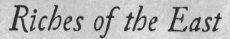
Riches of the East

News of Tew's raid spread to other pirates. They realized that Asia and Africa were a treasure hunter's paradise. Delicate silks, sparkling gems, rare spices, and smooth ivory were plentiful there.

The Red Sea soon became a favorite place for pirates. Pirate ships sailed around the small sea and attacked the slow-moving merchant ships.

Pirate ships chased down and robbed the Great Mogul's ships of their treasure.

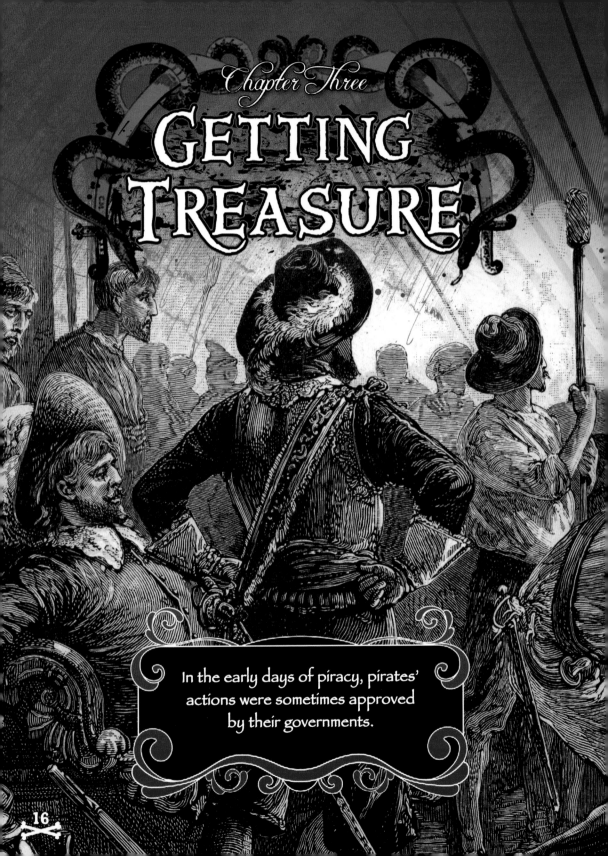

Chapter Three
GETTING TREASURE

In the early days of piracy, pirates' actions were sometimes approved by their governments.

With gold and jewels sailing in wooden ships, it's no surprise there were so many pirates. In the 1600s and early 1700s, many merchant ships were robbed at sea. What is surprising is who did the robbing and who knew about it.

Piracy with Permission

Some people were allowed to rob ships. They were called privateers. During wartime, rulers of countries like England and France gave a few sea captains documents called letters of marque. These letters promised the captains that they would not be punished for robbing enemy ships.

Learn About:
- Privateers
- False flags
- Blackbeard

By the early 1700s, many wars in Europe were over. Privateers were no longer allowed to rob ships. The peace was good for most people, but it was bad for privateers. They had no work and no money. Many privateers returned to robbing ships. These sailors were now illegal pirates.

Flying False Colors

On the ocean, it was difficult for merchant ships to tell friends from enemies. The captain of a merchant ship usually flew his country's flag. The flag told other ships where the merchant ship was from, but it also helped many pirates steal treasure.

The Barbary corsairs were famous pirates who sailed in the Mediterranean Sea. These pirates used false flags to lure ships loaded with treasure. Their favorite targets were Dutch ships. As they approached a Dutch ship, the corsairs flew a Dutch flag from their mast. When the two ships pulled alongside each other, the corsairs dropped the Dutch flag and raised their pirate flag.

Many times, the Dutch crew was too stunned to fight back when they saw the pirate flag. The corsairs boarded the Dutch ship and easily took their treasure. This trick was called "flying false colors." It was a good way to get treasure without a big fight.

Brothers Aruj and Kheir-ed-din Barbarossa were two of the most famous Barbary corsairs.

Just the sight of Blackbeard was enough to make merchant ship captains surrender.

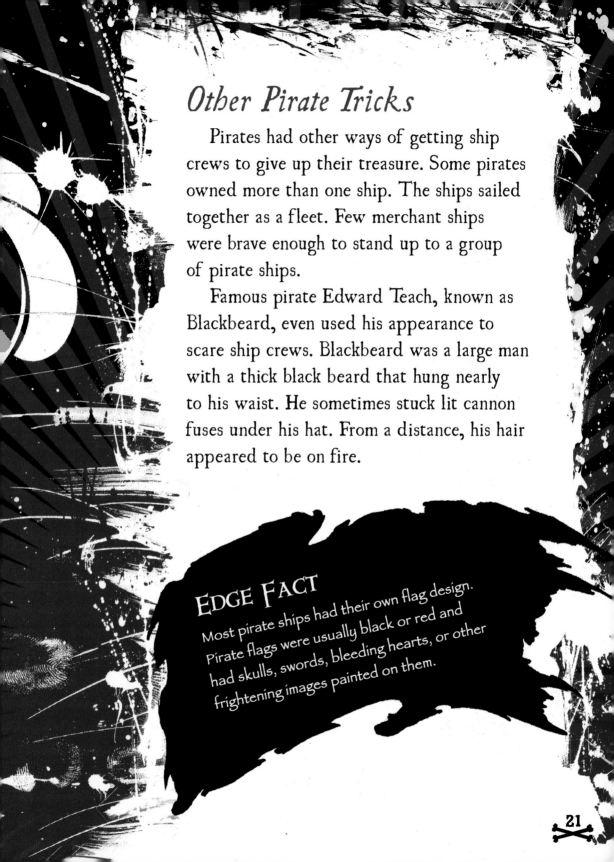

Other Pirate Tricks

Pirates had other ways of getting ship crews to give up their treasure. Some pirates owned more than one ship. The ships sailed together as a fleet. Few merchant ships were brave enough to stand up to a group of pirate ships.

Famous pirate Edward Teach, known as Blackbeard, even used his appearance to scare ship crews. Blackbeard was a large man with a thick black beard that hung nearly to his waist. He sometimes stuck lit cannon fuses under his hat. From a distance, his hair appeared to be on fire.

EDGE FACT

Most pirate ships had their own flag design. Pirate flags were usually black or red and had skulls, swords, bleeding hearts, or other frightening images painted on them.

Taverns were favorite places for pirates to spend their money.

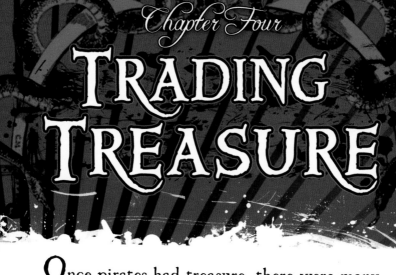

Chapter Four

TRADING TREASURE

Once pirates had treasure, there were many things they could do with it. Few pirates hung onto their gold for very long.

Pirate Parties

Pirates spent months on damp, crowded ships. Once they reached a city, all they wanted to do was have a good time. Most pirates spent their money quickly on alcohol and gambling.

Some towns along the American coast welcomed the pirates. Pirates sold goods for lower prices than those charged by the English. Plus, pirates arrived into harbors needing food and water, and they had the gold to pay for it.

Learn About:
- Fate of treasure
- Pirate towns
- Treasure hunting today

Towns like Newport, Rhode Island, and Bath, North Carolina, were popular pirate hangouts. But after a time, townspeople grew tired of the pirates' rowdy behavior. By the mid-1700s, most colonial towns refused to let pirate ships into their harbors.

Treasure Trend

In the late 1600s and early 1700s, owning a piece of pirate treasure was popular. Jade statues, ivory sculptures, and silk fans were displayed in some of the finest houses in the colonies.

EDGE FACT

In 1718, North Carolina governor Charles Eden made a deal with Blackbeard. He pardoned the pirate and his crew in exchange for a share of any treasure they stole.

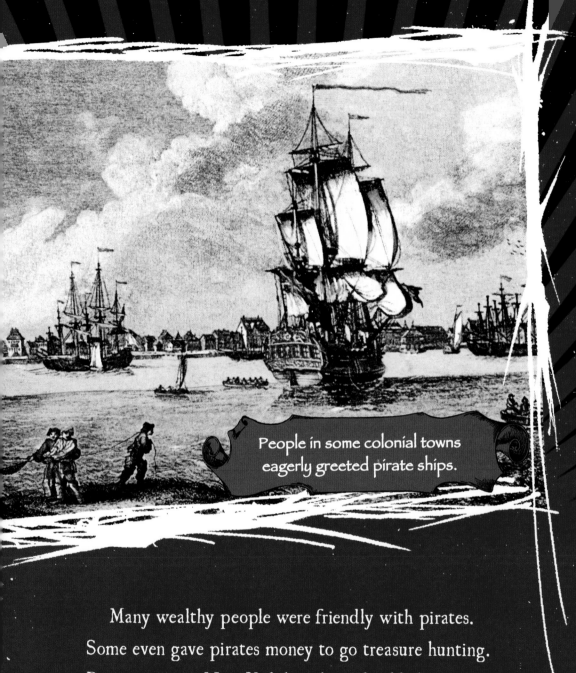

People in some colonial towns eagerly greeted pirate ships.

Many wealthy people were friendly with pirates. Some even gave pirates money to go treasure hunting. Businessmen in New York bought and sold the treasure that pirates brought.

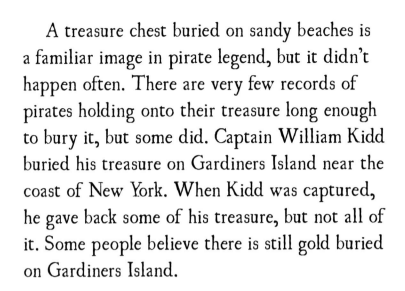

A treasure chest buried on sandy beaches is a familiar image in pirate legend, but it didn't happen often. There are very few records of pirates holding onto their treasure long enough to bury it, but some did. Captain William Kidd buried his treasure on Gardiners Island near the coast of New York. When Kidd was captured, he gave back some of his treasure, but not all of it. Some people believe there is still gold buried on Gardiners Island.

People still dream of finding pirate treasure chests filled with gold and jewelry.

Some pirate treasure ended up at the bottom of the ocean. Storms caused many pirate ships to sink, taking the riches with them. One of the most famous pirate shipwrecks happened in 1717. Pirate Sam Bellamy's ship the *Whydah* crashed into rocks off Cape Cod, Massachusetts. In 1984, divers found the wreck of the *Whydah*. It still held coins, cannons, and pieces from a game that the pirates had played.

Sea of the ...lands

Treasure Map

August 4, 1754

28

Treasure is one of the few things to survive from the days when pirates sailed the seas. Today, gold coins and other treasures stolen by pirates are found in museums around the world. With each piece of treasure, researchers learn more about the real world of pirates.

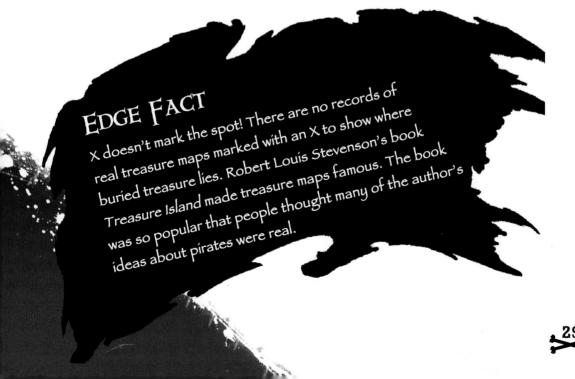

EDGE FACT

X doesn't mark the spot! There are no records of real treasure maps marked with an X to show where buried treasure lies. Robert Louis Stevenson's book Treasure Island made treasure maps famous. The book was so popular that people thought many of the author's ideas about pirates were real.

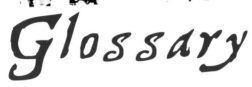

Glossary

cargo (KAR-goh)—the goods carried by a ship

colonist (KOL-uh-nist)—a person living in an area that is ruled by another country

fleet (FLEET)—a group of ships

loot (LOOT)—stolen goods or treasure

navigation (NAV-uh-gay-shun)—using instruments and charts to find your way in a ship or other vehicle

privateer (prye-vuh-TEER)—a person who owns a ship licensed to attack and steal from other ships

rowdy (ROU-dee)—noisy and wild

Read More

Davis, Kelly. *Pirates.* See-through. Philadelphia: Running Press Kids, 2003.

Meltzer, Milton. *Piracy & Plunder: A Murderous Business.* New York: Dutton, 2001.

Scott, Caitlin. *Treasure Hunting: Looking for Lost Riches.* High Five Reading. Mankato, Minn.: Capstone Press, 2004.

Internet Sites

FactHound offers a safe, fun way to find Internet sites related to this book. All of the sites on FactHound have been researched by our staff.

Here's how:

1. Visit *www.facthound.com*

2. Choose your grade level.

3. Type in this book ID **0736864288** for age-appropriate sites. You may also browse subjects by clicking on letters, or by clicking on pictures and words.

4. Click on the **Fetch It** button.

FactHound will fetch the best sites for you!

Index